COUNTDOWN TO DEMOCRACY

Copyright © Deborah French Frisher 2024
All rights reserved

First published by Galileo Books
ISBN 978-0-913123-46-1

Cover design by Coral Black

Book design by Adam Robinson
for GoodBookDevelopers.com

COUNTDOWN

TO

DEMOCRACY

Deborah French Frisher

GALILEO PRESS

*Dedicated to
the ancestors of hope, joy, and peaceful democracy,
my children Lila Rose & Trevor, Luke & Emily,
newborns on the way,
and all our neighbors and kin*

CONTENTS

Day 52.	Shutter	1
Day 51.	Jack-o-lanterns	3
Day 50.	Heresy	4
Day 49.	Hemoglobin	6
Day 48.	Anti-inflammatory	7
Day 47.	Industry	8
Day 46.	Ambition	9
Day 45.	Capitalism	10
Day 44.	Voter	11
Day 43.	Detonate	12
Day 42.	Gentlewoman	13
Day 41.	Produce	14
Day 40.	Pestilence	15
Day 39.	Parenting	16
Day 38.	Everybody	17
Day 37.	Concepts	18
Day 36.	Separation	19
Day 35.	Motherland	20
Day 34.	Nurture	21
Day 33.	Beachfront	22
Day 32.	Unbanned	23
Day 31.	Conspiracy	24
Day 30.	Infantile	25
Day 29.	Inter-being	27
Day 28.	Posers	28
Day 27.	Encampments	29
Day 26.	Needlepoint	30
Day 25.	Blindside	31
Day 24.	Elders	32

Day 23.	Prescience	33
Day 22.	Executioner	34
Day 21.	Witness	35
Day 20.	Puppetry	36
Day 19.	Testimony	37
Day 18.	Patriarchy	38
Day 17.	Gaps	39
Day 16.	Cosmic	41
Day 15.	Allegiance	42
Day 14.	Peace	43
Day 13.	Earth	44
Day 12.	Cause	45
Day 11.	Commemoration	46
Day 10.	Natural	47
Day 9.	Disarming	48
Day 8.	Upscale	49
Day 7.	Vision	50
Day 6.	Phases	51
Day 5.	Blankets	52
Day 4.	Prayer	53
Day 3.	Flesh	54
Day 2.	Everyday	55
Day 1.	Birthing	56
Epilogue.	Cannonball	59

Acknowledgments & Appreciations	*65*
About the Author	*66*

Day 52. Shutter

America has a point of view problem.
Ask any photographer, polishing their lens.

We thought we fooled the cosmic picture,
taking selfies with the stars,
pointing & shooting
past the poor for more
small human footprints,
big puffy boot of mankind
on the neck of the moon.

History is looking at democracy,
never being shown the whole truth.

Lifting sightline,
a wide-angle shutters into reframe:
a spherical aquamarine planet,
involving & resolving ardency
towards an intimate gravitas
down-streaming in our veins,
blood river-running with the water keepers.

Throw open the windows
and King of Diamond doors!

This country has the Grand Canyon,
and oxygen is fresh air there.

How much are who, perhaps, you,
maybe, we are going to care,
zooming in for a close up?

Day 51. Jack-o-lanterns

How do we carve
this whole pumpkin
to glow inside itself for the light?

If only, together, we might.

A man holds up his handwritten sign with the Seven Diamond
dollar. You can't un-hear his call for help into the silence of
 passers-by, everybody's shame echoing, shhhh, shame on
 who,
the city's shark teeth, scraping the skyline.

Day 50. Heresy

As for public education,
we're not born knowing
how to solve an equity equation.
Some people learn
 how to un-teach love.

The cowardly
 decide to make up things:
"If god loves us,
he won't cause a
climate change,
it's in the book of books,
there have always been
storms." But the lights have gone out.

Children can see the dementors—
wrong flashes in hurricane eyes.
Some grown-ass Jack of Spades
has locked a child in their room.
Profane preachers reach out for
riches with gun glory pitches,
and whatever else secrets please.

Fans roar for a touchdown,
 pledging allegiance to concussions.
"What's a fracture?" they say,
"We're the USA!"

Helmets to hearts,
they suffer repercussions.

Others have seen bombs bursting
where children can hardly breathe.
Until justice is played
on the home field,
the brave take a knee.

Day 49. *Hemoglobin*

Most people got used to it,
holding their breath. Trauma triggered
Eight dance Clubs dead. Packing heat
is no code for handsomeness.

The gunman ends it all,
broken by psych ops code,
blood splattering for the exits,
marking hate as the official issue again.

Day 48. Anti-inflammatory

"What is love?"
the Queen asks the King of Hearts.

"Love is lifelong wonder
at regenerative arts."

Foraging for a lion's mane,
distant green sleeves wave in the breeze.

Day 47. *Industry*

The asphalt road leads but no one wants to take it,
heat-waving memories of labor serving time,
cars broken as yesterday's promise in Detroit.

The plastic profits suck
from bottled water,
child-size bullet proof
vests are selling &
coal is coming back
in every woman's blue stockings,
cinched with purity rings around the knees,
while big suits go unzipped on shrunken men,
pissing petroleum in the park, frack them,
going with giddy-up
to the twirlie-girlie shows.

And if anybody gets hurt
or hit with a Four of Clubs along the way,
the greedy like to say from insured cubicles,
it's a pre-existing condition.

Saying the words "thoughts & prayers"
are the new trick.
There is no treat in this.

Day 46. Ambition

The glitterati hands out soggy boxes
to live in while the escalator loops upward
to the firmament floor, please,
into the Six of Club doors, squeeze,
every applicant wanting to be
a star in digi-management.

Day 45. Capitalism

Common ordinary sense people
have a right to be bitter.

Most folks never get near
the promise of things on tv,
so there must be a hidden enemy
in the Five of Diamond market theories.

Day 44. Voter

Can we make the river run clear again,
scatter the barcode brawl hackers,
show the touchscreen punks
there is nothing to hide from the pillow man?

Ours is the freedom of balloting
human rights, picking justice squarely
with Eighth note changes,
marked for posterity, mailed for security.

Each one person, fairly casts one vote.

That's the problem with dismissing
the atrocity of a law called Citizens
United, A misnamed misinforming
treason of human reason,
designed to make a mockery of democracy.

Day 43. Detonate

Postal terror is the Ace of Spade
of a racist pipe bomb.

No church organ plays at the corner smokes store.

She's "a bombshell"
is a patriarchal pipe dream,
sagging with insult in his flaccid mirror.

Day 42. Gentlewoman

"I ain't afraid."

People find their ears to hear the Queen of Heart.

Day 41. Produce

So many personal opines feeling this &
that, chat their wits into twotes,
sounding off rants,
or branding to seduce,
processing everything, no time
in the daily grind to find fresh cilantro.

Day 40. Pestilence

Where have all the farmers gone?
They are Two Spades of a blockhead
down from that factory in town
on your right, can't miss the sign,
says "Hazardous Chemicals,"
past the hospital where migrant
mothers wheezing go
 with heaving breath to die.

Day 39. *Parenting*

Other mothers shudder
over the fatality of peanut butter,
packing kiddo lunches
in the shade of the NRA.

It's easier to buy a gun than a trombone.

Is that man at the school crossing
with his Three of Clubs case
long enough for an AK-47
going to bring out his bass
for the children today?

Is that somebody's dad swinging
the instrument bag? Will he teach them
how he loves to play jazz?

Day 38. Everybody

We need to pry open the flawed idea
behind the elegant design,

liberation is not insta-individuation.

Democracy's freedom is an all-together thing.

Day 37. Concepts

Schools teach, some cringers preach sex ed, shrill
ranters sound ugly on venereal disease & sex
before marriage facts, mostly fictions,

while steeling themselves inside
silver-plated promises and porn addictions.

Across the pasture
in another middle school,
students draw pastels,
soft strokes on slate:
phallus of hummingbird beak,
womb of butterfly wings.

Day 36. Separation

The border fence surrounds a playground
where the American flag is raised
for each public detention day.

You can't see the chain links on freedom
around the baseball Four of Diamond
through the vine with its fading yellow bells
the children ring for a drop of sweetness,
to quench their honey-suckling thirst.

Day 35. Motherland

Shaking the key in the brown girl's face,
the pale hand of power
keeps wanting more from kids.

"Door's locked,"
lips pinched from inside the uniform.

Immigrant parents are barred away,
their flesh-and-blood children
guarded by chicken wire,
Ten feet of barbed Spades.

Homeland security scans the facility, humming
lullabies to concentration camp.

And the evangelicals are far away,
singing, "Jesus loves the little children,
all the children of the world."

Day 34. Nurture

One boy is left without a question,
overheated on the border,
stealing to feed his dying mother
the last crust of bread.

Day 33. Beachfront

Other children laugh a lot
and run on American sand
with hands they've used all day to make
castles, digging their Jack of Spades
to shape wet bricks for blocks,
building towers beside fish ashore
dead from plastic wishes
in the overheated sea,
happy barefoot toddlers
calling their pockets snack holes.

Day 32. Unbanned

Mercy with her Ace of Heart library
cart serves the public good.

Day 31. Conspiracy

Firstborn son-of-a-gun rises from a tanning
bed, bleat-tweets "my father"
and the room clears Mar-a-Lago.

Back in DC, limos line in Nines of
Spades, parking crime-planning meetings
inside the capitol garage, hiding in plain
day, where boys who are proud
met oaths without reason,
vowing to keep treason current.

Day 30. *Infantile*

Humidity is the best revenge in Florida.
An old man wipes orange foundation
 from his plucked elder brow,
roasting white marshmallows
on his gold-plated bayonet,
claiming his secret sauce
is under-worn diplomacy.

He is wanting nothing more
than a massive stupidity
to oath his swear upon.

A goldbar thug huckster,
with used up titles:
former, mocked, president
begging for more, & more & more.

Thunder cracks up skies
like the brains of bigots
in a frying pan when they
realize how hate words
sizzle out to nothing good,
nothing better than a hard-cooked monument
bronze man pulled over from his pedestal, chiseled
chin in the mud—colonial or confederate—
facedown in the throb of a geodesic wound.

Sticky as a pedophile's candy,
the infant tyrant wipes his smeared
face, feeling nothing, sneering,
badly acting befuddled by anyone
left insulted & offended.

Day 29. Inter-being

The moral of the story is pet pending.
If we elect an inhumane president
who doesn't put a pet dog
nor a good book in the White House,
we're going to see "go mean" fast
with a misfit Joker.

Day 28.   Posers

Corner store dreams shattering in Kentucky,
close as Nine billy Clubs away,
nothing human left, only ammo.

Mazel Tov gets murdered in Philly's temple.

The ghost of President past
rides in a golf cart chariot,
his shapely apron of a wife
bending over steroid stilettos
for her anti-close up,
serving her country
a soothing belladonna
until we're tipsy in her shoes
with the presidential seal
embossed on her heels,
then we'd be best not to notice
how he lost the election,
how his putter petered out.

We vote because sometimes,
nonsense is a cruel vanity,
and the future needs our thoroughgoing love.

Day 27. *Encampments*

Outdoor outfitters balance their books
from the tents gone missing–
the homeless & refugees below the line
against the margins of product moved
for happy family camping
in privatized public parks.

One child hugs a tree,
another dreams of owning
the thing for timber.

A pocket knife slices the rosy apple skin,
its core, a star ship of seeds.

Others are said to be rotten
when the misbegotten fail to thrive.

We've arrived at the end of our mercy,
tired & burned out on doing the winner-takes-all things.

Day 26. *Needlepoint*

A shoot-out needles the urban concrete.

Talking morning head shows,
everybody stirring to a state of
the fentanyl shakes before breakfast,
small-minding tweet sculpts,
white bred bigly insults,
cable news pussy-grab struts
crossing patriotic platforms on digital display.

Jawboning slackers of American democracy
loose-lip their finger-wagging liberty,
tightening the future's blindfold
they promised their ole' lady
liberty would look sexy thin,
boys just being boys again,
men with double-butter chins
not looking anyone in the eye,
not really caring under which tarp
America is currently starving.

Day 25. *Blindside*

"Thank you for your service."

"There are no words,"
 an infantry grunt growls
 from inside the good soldier,
 his Jack of purple Heart medal
 live-streamed for the nation,
 his children left stateside,
 while his wife gets deported.

A man in fatigues is diagnosable,
 short-sighted military complex:
 he followed orders, dutifully,
 plowing pastures into minefields
 to protect the homeland.

Years go by, wilds green up again,
 children running to catch the ball
 in the blinding sun last seen
 throwing up their hands.

Day 24. Elders

A grown man sleeps on sidewalk, leans
up against the wall beneath an awning
under the sign, United Liquors, lit up,
vetting the streets. It's peacetime.

Uptown inside her embattled financials,
an unemployed woman with pewter hair
jokes behind the glass with the teller
that her silver life is a rat race
from bank to that liquor store
and back to the bank & more.

"Stressed like a six-pack of Red Bulls,"
she says, "Nobody wants
to hire a woman over forty,
over thirty-five, make that,
yeah, thirty-five, that's pretty accurate."

Again, she says, to be precise, "pretty."

Day 23. Prescience

The high school gang bang
to Supreme Court pipeline
is not rusting well, according
to another woman who remembers things,
Anita Hill, so brave.

Day 22. Executioner

Meanwhile, the lady senator
from Maine with no comment
on Roe vs Wade is on her way
to the top of the fold,
making headlines out of indecision,
her undecided, not deciding,
photobombing The New York Times.

Day 21. Witness

To the end of time, a woman lawyer is
testifying the violation, protocol ripping open
patriarchy's empty skull,
her small pelvis & large spirit,
crushed as collateral
in a high school drinking game.

She tells the story of their bad boy
glory, monotone in front of
microphones
on Capitol Hill. Keyboard
percussion taps out from clickbait,
unlocks the rooms she locked
her worst terrors in,
a shrill cost of silence,
echoing sister screams in chambers
unseen by social media witnesses.

Across town, a living room
gathering of clutched pearls,
drowning thirsts for tenderness
with a pill here, a jigger there,
wanting to forget something,
playing favorites to sugar daddy
husbands, busting out rhinestone &
sapphire chokers with sparklers for
earrings, hearts bought by Jacks
with double-butter chins.

Day 20. *Puppetry*

Whose divine hand
pulls the strings to her ovaries?
Will we outsmart, on November Six of Heart,
mega slogans for womanly self-loathing?

Bleached blonde citizens for a united
cover-up with roots of dark envies & petty
bad in bedness of their puffy-assed men,
refusing to look at how their own whiteness might be
gaming affirmative action again & again
and how that affects the sisters of color?

Day 19. Testimony

Unprecedented finger tapping tell-alls
are scrolling down from women's lives,
exposing their trembling again for social cause.

And it's no Queen of Diamond wonder—
without safety or justice,
what is left, but to confess
primal horror in status updates?

Each act of saving face
from social media disgrace
is to dunk herself in society's tub of shame,
and if isolation doesn't drown her, they say,
she's a weird witch & unsuitable
for church or work or love.

Branding is the cure-all,
post-feminist & guiltless,
("Isn't she lovely?"),
pronounced dead & innocent,
pure as an algorithm.

Day 18. Patriarchy

Epics ago in a forest on an island,
a young girl picked up a rough bark stick
and tipped it, dipped it
in rain-puddle mush.

Round & looping, her hand began
expressing impressions before she was
clubbed, Ace-axed in her heart.

Her teenage dream got frozen
in the before times, midway through
the long hormone-blasted tunnel.

Her life is a Venn diagram
of overlapping systems
and she had been left out
of the interlocking cliques, trembling.
In another time, she might have been
a journalist.

Day 17. Gaps

Can the bridges in nature's blueprints
be the ones we engineer— a fallen redwood
across the creek, free-ranging children,
honing their barefoot balance?

A gran in Georgia flips a pancake breakfast,
dips her Black fingers in olive oil at the door
to bless each child with a sign of the cross,
school mornings before grammar
taught by supremacist white rules.

It's a fair question:
whose history is told in school as real,
and whose true story is left out of it?

An immense gulf exists between
honorable infantry headstones
engraved by a wartime nation
and hopeful composting
for fruit bearing regeneration.

Forever-chemical gulfs remain
between wealth tax cuts
and petty penalties for outliers.

There is a teachers-can't-live-
where-their-students-can gulf;
a gulf between wages for women & men,
between rents where techies & artists live.

There's a dead zone
between mortality rates
for mothers by race
with gulfs of health care between them.

A gulf of communication divides generations,
a chasm between civil rights & human greed
in the gulf between gerrymandering
and fair vote democracy.

A gorge cuts between the anthem
& tender for its dollar note,
trenches dug between gun-and-god lockstep,
and a kind, disarming hope.

Day 16. *Cosmic*

The largest crater is on the surface of our minds:
pallid conquerors stand on the perimeter,
while first peoples have been kicked in.

Racists prefer their own kind,
armed up to the Two of Spades,
refusing to make amends with anybody
who might be different from them.

To begin again, why not consider reparations?
No one prepares for that, not the same way,
not with the same industry they apply toward apocalypse.

The pursuit of happiness depends on a civic kind of love
with health care for all, as if each life depends upon it
because we do -- ask any epidemiologist.

Look up! Decentralize yourself.

A dog star hangs
nearby the planet
brightning an indigo night,
honey-mooning, hankering to be consummate,
with human feeling,
one dot bright on a horizon striped by cosmos,
lit more spectacular
by aging flame-throwers, twirling
and spill-tossing light years.

Day 15. Allegiance

I pledge this Eight of a poet's Heart
to an equity experiment, all in,
toward multicultural resources,
divergent without exception,
and with liberty & justice
toward a culture of belonging like kin.

Day 14. Peace

Remembering the ocean,
she went there often
with her Two of Heart view,
through all kinds of climate
change, to recall her pacific.

Day 13. Earth

Before nations, desire flamed on flower
wicks, a tonic of heat, form discovering
spark, enduring brilliance
buried beneath a mountain of
particulars and pressures,
raw & uneven,

in oblivious beauty,

sand everlasting as Two
Diamonds, unseen & unknown,
covalent, apolitical, primeval.

Day 12. Cause

A child you might know holds a seed,
learning to make their impression on the world,
finger-pushing in the garden for real,
nestling in starts for wild flowers,
dirt down with a free hand.
A flip of the wrist, along the row,
another seed is pressed in again.
Left to its own nature,
winter rains back to us in blossoms.
Lovers will close the shades,
find out they are not blind,
seeing each other through a warm spring night
in their arms on Cranberry Island.

Day 11. *Commemoration*

The park bench is still there,
and the tree where an Eight of Diamond
heart is embossed on a brass plate
set in the ground
above the tree's living roots,
in the shade of its crown.

The people appealed to the state
for the love-etched plate
that is being unwrapped today,

Rangers pulling down caution tape,
after something political.

Protests had stopped
the big underground scheme
to be fracking up the place.

Then came the militia, like a psych ward,
jagged mental jaws
with locked & loaded feelings
pumped up disorder, marching out of step.

A weathering Marine cap & a bridal bouquet
were placed close by, a child's toy squirt fish
tucked in the peeling bark of eucalyptus.

Day 10. *Natural*

What good is it all when your solid rock
falls, shaken by Ten of Spades rage and
despair?

I toss a stone in the air,
gravity throws it back, a breakdown crunch.

Pieces. It's all in pieces,
a geode that formed under
pressure, charged jagged lightning
after concentrated waiting,
trying to hold open some space
inside for brilliance-making,
while the seasons crowded in
and having succeeded, then,
this crack open. A glistening
explodes from a secret chandelier
inside a plodding clod of clay.
On such a clumsy day as this,
I believe in geology,
how it flickers with love again,

and the earth & I are engaged!

Day 9. Disarming

The Queen of Spade is a mushroom now.
See what explodes in your mind's eye
and how?

It is the love of the question
that turns into science,
the dignity of mycorrhizal,
water & roots, signifying
inter-soul beneath the toadstool.

The Queen of Spade is a mushroom now.
lifting the verdant veil she wore,
dancing with mycelium after the wildfire,
refreshing the forest floor.

Or her shadow can be a citizen fail,
a responsibility drop,
the nuclear family failure
to show up at your ballot box.

Femme fatale with your AR-15:
reimagine yourself, mushroom queen.

Day 8. Upscale

Gents at bus stops– it all seems the next best thing
till it happens to your block of the woods,
timber felling politics in the rainforest,
the next oily war raging abroad,
a well-refined plot. Of course, they say
it's not happening, in the streets with the word
going down, "Hands up, don't shoot!"
and all we ever want is, "arms out, hug me."

Day 7. Vision

A ladder stands in the vineyard,
with its twenty-five rungs, the top
close enough to reach out
and scoop handfuls of billowing sky.

A bluesy sea glass heart clears
from inside a silverfish cloud.

Day 6. Phases

The moon is a strand of pearls
thread faithfully together
while the barn owl hoots,
a curve of opal swirls,
dancing with solitude
inside an abalone shell.

At Three Diamonds past
midnight, democracy is still
possible.

Day 5. Blankets

Elections ought to be
a day off the job,
stirring some neighborly love
in the melting soup of differences.

A democratic chorus, native
peoples, with Hamlets & Ophelias
moving in, naturalized Desdemonas
& Othellos, raising the Ten despairs
to the power of Hearts in asylum,
a patchwork of state shapes
quilted into a belonging,
weighted with nightmare comforters,
warming the chilling winter violence
toward tomorrow's dream of verdancy
cast by our votes.

Day 4. Prayer

On Sunday, Seventh of church Club day
before we begin to grind the coffee again,
we eat democracy for brunch,
our noses in the morning paper screens.

After Saturday night's wishes
rendered in French kisses,
tossing laurel crowns tipsy
on love's spearing tongue,
grief is catching up with us,
for what this country might have been,
sorrow for what it never was.
Ready as moral Monday & the justice rush,
this Sunday, we shush for the mystic.

Day 3. Flesh

Two of Hearts face each other
with quivers of longing & dread:
"Might it all come together if
my soul meets your body instead?"

Day 2. Everyday

"These are anthuriums," said the lab coat with a man in it.

"No, they are called love lace & painter's palette," said his wife.

"Anyway, I brought seven with roots home for you."
"Why seven, why not more or less?"

"Seven for the notes that had to be played
 before we could change up the octave."
 He picked up his mandolin.

"I see seven valentines,
 rouge teases with golden flames,
 or are they speaking in tongues,
 outstanding in the autumn burnish,
 preferring to lick clean air
 than to make a show of it?" she
 asked, placing blossoms in the
 window.

"How can you be so cheerful
 now?" he tensed
 two days before the vote.
"
 I don't know how we can do it
 under hateful conditions," and then,

 she took his hand,
 and they began to hold each other's love, again.

Day 1. Birthing

Election day, we sign our true names
from the persons in us that we would be
before the star-borne circumstance.

Before we are America's sons or daughters,
we are pure rhythm & motion
in guileless chambers of the heart,
and nothing less than that will turn us on.

We tune in to the exit poll's play-by-play,
all day in long lines,
each waiting for their chance to be counted.

Out of the pundit mental hacksaws,
nerve-wracking racist jackhammers,
suddenly, something beautiful
fluttering, rippling like a shimmy of hope,
harmonics from Nine Heart-shaped faces,
sing-songs from cupid-bow lips.

"Can I make my heart stronger, not a stranger?"

America, we can hear you.

The forest tree is ringing in our ears.
Is that the seabird calling me or the bee?

The motherland
is not somewhere out there,
fantastical & far,
but intimate as the dew
on the first peoples' earth,
taken for granted
underneath a patriotic picnic.

The family of humanity are
free-willing, collective,
organic, planetary, & wilding.
We labor and deliver democracy—
urgent as the newborn's cry for kin.

Epilogue. Cannonball

I don't know what to say to you, America.
You let me down & you funked me up
with your messing around—
swing & ragtime dancing,
ballrooms & the rodeo,
swimsuit competitions & editions,
string bikinis & theories,
chaos breaking like cue balls
racked up in triangles.

The whole point is life begins when
the tight fit from a mold
breaks open, tumbles into,
bumps together, opens up, America!

Your flag waves to me before
it's folded away ceremoniously
with formal white gloves,
before folks bust open
the bloody red bar-b-cue sauce,
everything laid to rest with honors,
so much we don't talk about now.

To even mention happiness
as an organizing principle
for forming a nation
was a clever ambition
toward eating & sleeping together.

You are mine to belong to,
you in the star-spangled sequins,
a punk country rocker,
your legacy is clay & heat lightning,
banjo & drum, today a marching band!

Soldiers soldiers soldiers
consigned to some cause far away
that outlives me to protect
who I would love were I to know them.

The smug has eaten the feel-good now:
I know how much can go wrong,
the compulsive covid washing
of shopping hands on President's Day.

Vanities drive the capital, hawking
value-packed self-loathing, not expecting
the glitter & grit to turn into a sightglass.
Focusing that lens seems to get you closer,
while what you see is so far, far away.

Patriotic fireworks pop in my brain.

Who recalls before all the asphalt came
where the red road crested
an indigenous belonging most cannot name?—
before railroad tracks were laid
in brown & black blues singing for the motherland.

It's a clash—how do we live with it?—
democracy's wish for happy, before sober
reparations are made on Juneteenth?

I am imperfect in my love for you, America,
I can't bear the responsibility on my shoulders
and you can bear nothing at all if I remain silent
on your birthday, it's July! Momma's apples
are dropping from all the branches into pies.

Sons of yearning
are making love to daughters
of green renaissance,
revolution buzzing,
the honey queen bees in busy hives,
urgent with transfiguring survival's
sting into a thriving sweetness.

This is your song America—transcendental,
everything's-a-musical on Broadway, Billie Holiday,
Herbie Hancock, & Elvis' blue suede shoes.

I got this howling inspiration
from a Ginsberg poet and my appreciation
is to—note a different spelling & no relation—
Supreme Court Justice Ginsburg
who delivered the docket
for a woman's life in lockdown.

My fellow citizens,
I'm want to bake

a re-birth day cake
to the nation & light
candles on top of it
with the match of desire
striking up the heat of a wish
for everyone's free bird.
Swim meets & clear water lakes,
diving boards, the run, a jump
off the edge, America–
I'll never grow past
holding out my tongue to catch
the splash that you can make!

VOTE!

Resources for Action

For Voting Information in Your State:
VOTE.GOV

League of Women Voters:
VOTE411.ORG

Acknowledgments & Appreciations

Shouting out loving praise to Agnes Cerhati for her
 encouragement and editorial eagle eye and to Lindsay
 Lusby for her keen poetry expertise & developmental
 support with these poems. All respect with thanksgiving
 for Barrett Warner at Galileo Press. Marking a coda
 of thank-you's to Michael Papenburg for his talented
 musical improvisations and accompaniment for these
 poems in their day-by-day release. Armfuls of gratitude
 to Madi Harbauer for her social media direction. Armfuls
 of appreciation to Ron Law for his consulting friendship
 every civic and literary step along my way toward
 publication and democratic action.

Proceeds from the sale of this book will be donated to
March For Our Lives, MARCHFOROURLIVES.ORG

About the Author

Deborah French Frisher is a poet, screenwriter, and playwright. She held an early career position in the Carter Administration as liason between the White House and the Council on Wage & Price Stability. She was a Littauer Fellow at Harvard University's Kennedy School of Government. Her poems have appeared or are forthcoming in *Writers Resist*, *Quail Bell Magazine*, and *Book of Matches*. Her not-for-profit Neighborly Project provides arts-based interventions toward social justice and community mental health. A former educator at the California Institute of Integral Studies School for Counseling Psychology, she lives in the San Francisco Bay Area.